how to think about how you think

identity, inquiry, evolution, and the risk of thinking you know

JEFF CARREIRA

how to think
about
how you think

identity, inquiry, evolution, and
the risk of thinking you know

JEFF CARREIRA

EMERGENCE EDUCATION
Philadelphia, Pennsylvannia

ISBN: 978-1-954642-20-1

Emergence Education
P.O. Box 63767
Philadelphia, PA 19147
EmergenceEducation.com

Original cover art by Jeff Carreira
Cover and interior design by Sophie Peirce

Printed in the United States of America.

"Don't just read this book – think about it. "

— JEFF CARREIRA

Contents

Introduction

THIS BOOK'S AIM IS to demonstrate the profound utility of philosophy. It is rooted in the conviction that philosophy is not a luxury—it is a necessity that none of us can afford to ignore.

This is not an instruction manual for inquiry or a collection of philosophical ideas that I want you to adopt. I haven't written it in order to tell you what to think. I wrote it to give you some interesting and important things to think about. In doing this I'm following a romantic sentiment that recognizes that the true value of writing lies beyond the literal understanding contained in the words and can only be found in the truth that is provoked in your own heart and mind by the words. Spurring the reader to new insight and understanding is the ultimate measure of a writer's success. Ralph Waldo Emerson, one of the first American men of letters, similarly insisted that truth and real understanding must be birthed within us and not merely accepted from the understanding of others:

> *"Truly speaking, it is not instruction, but provocation, that I can receive from another soul."*

I have organized this book around four provocative statements:

- The world is not the way you think it is.
- You may not be who you think you are.
- We don't know, yet we have to act as if we do.
- The circumstances around us are changing faster than we can.

Each of these statements is presented as a good reason to think deeply about how you think. The book is divided into four parts according to these statements. Each part begins with one of the statements above. The statement is followed by a few sentences that create a framework for your contemplation about it, and then two or three short essays, concluding with a few sentences of final contemplation.

Each of the four parts offers an inquiry into a profound existential question. My advice is to read vulnerably, not analytically or critically. Each essay contained here is a snapshot, a glimpse into an extraordinary perspective on reality. They are seeds for contemplation, starting points for your own inquiry. Don't just read this book—think about it. Give less of your attention to the words on the page and more to where the words can take you. Follow your own curiosity and develop your own understanding. To quote Emerson again:

> *"The foregoing generations beheld God and nature face to face; we, through their eyes. Why should we not also enjoy an original relation to the universe?"*

My first intention in writing this book was to give you some interesting and important things to think about. My second objective is to educate you (especially if you happen to be an American) about some of the ideas that are part of the rich tradition of American philosophy, ideas that are very likely already embedded in the way you've learned to think.

The American character is diverse and somewhat contradictory, but one trait generally associated with it is pragmatism. Americans like things that work. That might be why the "love of philosophy" is not one of the characteristics most often associated with Americans. And it is probably not surprising that the greatest American philosophers have all insisted that philosophy is only worthwhile if it serves as a tool for living better lives and facing life's challenges.

The philosophical ideas most discussed in this book are those that were developed by the classical American philosophers Charles Sanders Peirce, William James, and John Dewey. These three brilliant minds were the originators of the philosophy called pragmatism, which remains to this day America's most significant contribution to world philosophy.

JEFF CARREIRA

PART ONE

The World is Not the Way You Think It Is

We look out at the world, and assume that's the way it is. It's not. The world may be the way it is, but our perception of it is seldom completely accurate and probably never will be. Knowing this is very important.

The following short essays illustrate how some great minds have addressed the challenge that our perception of the world may or may not have much to do with the way the world actually is.

CHAPTER ONE

The Myth of the Given

Does this mean that we select and are locked into the earlier discovery path? Can we improve it. Yes we can. Can we build a new one? Yes

OUR LIVES ARE GOVERNED by ideas. The way you see and respond to the world is as much a product of your beliefs about the world as anything else. The great American psychologist and philosopher William James realized this and taught that the most important capacity that human beings have is "the will to believe." James didn't think that we could choose our actions. He believed our actions were the result of the ideas we believed in. It may feel like we are choosing what to do, but in truth the range of options we have to choose from is limited by what we believe is possible and preferable, and that often leaves us with very little choice.

What we can do, James realized, is consciously choose which ideas we believe in. Those beliefs will inevitably unfold into action of their own accord, but at least we have exercised our will to believe and created the framework out of which our choices arise.

This book asks you to examine your beliefs. To discover what you actually know firsthand and what you have learned secondhand and take on faith. Most of us take more on faith than we realize. We all know, for instance, that the Earth revolves around the Sun. We learned that in elementary school. But do we actually have any direct evidence of it? If we look up at the sky, what we see is the Sun going around the Earth. We have been told that it is the other way around. We accept the truth of it and assume that someone has or has had direct evidence of it. We all believe many things that we accept on faith, and we assume that we have good reason to do so.

During the mid-twentieth century, the American philosopher Wilfrid Sellars opened a line of inquiry into the assumptions behind what we think we know. He gave a famous series of lectures about what he called "the myth of the given." The simplest way to understand what he was getting at is to say that the world is not always the way it appears to be. The world doesn't just exist; it appears to us, it shows up in our perception, and the way it appears is not necessarily the way it is. The world presents itself to us through layers of interpretation. William James talked about our experience of the world as being "thick"— thick with layers of meaning and significance that are ultimately interpretations of reality, not reality in an objective sense. If we don't recognize the ways that we are interpreting our experience, those interpretations simply become part of what we assume is real.

Most of us probably don't have a problem with this—after all, we all know that we don't always see things clearly. If we look deeply into how much of our experience of reality might actually be false, we most likely will reach a point where we don't want to ask anymore questions. At that point we can fall into two traps. One is the way of the fundamentalist, who tenaciously holds on to what he or she already believes to be true in spite of any evidence that might present itself to the contrary. The other trap is the way of the cynic, who concludes that there is ultimately no way to know what is true and gives up either trying and feels superior to anyone still foolish enough to believe they can figure anything out. The end result in both cases is that we give ourselves an excuse not to question any further and we break Charles Sanders Peirce's prime directive by blocking the road to inquiry.

This book is offering a different possibility—the way of perpetual inquiry. On this path of perpetual inquiry we don't see truth as an end point to settle into. We are not looking for an excuse to stop looking, because we see every discovered truth as a jumping-off point to further inquiry. Each discovery is a temporary stepping stone that offers just enough stability to launch us into the next inquiry and the next discovery of truth. On this path our questioning is not converging toward a final answer. It is opening up into the discovery of new questions to ask and new truths to be discovered — inquiry without end.

If we seriously consider the possibility of embarking wholeheartedly on a path of perpetual inquiry, we may find even more resistance arising. After all, we will think, you can't question everything forever. There has to be something real and solid and true somewhere that ends the questions. Questioning perpetually does not mean that there is no real truth. It just means that we can never be sure that we have found the real truth. It takes courage to remain open to new possibilities. We feel secure when we think we know the truth, uncertainty about what's true is frightening.

Whether we rest in what we know and defend it as true, or conclude that what we know is that there is no truth, we stop looking. We close down. I hope to convince you in this short book that closing down and assuming you know, is more dangerous than staying open and receptive to the possibility that you are wrong.

Another way to think about the myth of the given is as the deeply held belief that underneath the appearance of reality there is something that we can safely assume is actually real and true—something that is just given. This ground of truth is not something we need to question. This is the bedrock of our beliefs, the foundation that supports them all. As long as we assume that a foundation of truth exists to support our beliefs we feel like we are standing on solid ground.

Most of us first encountered the idea of "the given" in our high school physics classes. Remember? You start a physics problem with a list of givens. For instance, if you know the distance a car travels and the time it took to go that distance, you can calculate the average speed of the car. The basic idea is that as long as you know a sufficient number of initial facts you can use the rules of logic to derive new facts. The new facts will be true because they are based on previously known "givens" that we know are true.

In our everyday thinking we don't always realize what we are assuming to be "given." What we accept as real is built on a mountain of assumptions the size and scale of which we are almost entirely unaware of. The ideas and concepts that we know of are the tip of the iceberg—an island of thought that is reality just the tip of a mountain of assumptions that are hidden in the murky depths of the unconscious. These assumptions have built up over our own lifetime and throughout the history of the human mind.

As human understanding has been built up through centuries of thought, the ideas of one generation become the unconscious assumptions of the next. The process of discovery proceeds, generation after generation, age to age, leading right up to the ideas in our own minds. When we begin to realize how many assumptions lie behind our thinking, we start to wonder, as I believe Sellars and Descartes did, if there is anything truly underived and rock-solid true underneath it all. Maybe we are sitting on a mountain of assumptions, built on other assumptions, built on other assumptions, all the way to the bottom.

What we assume to be reality as we look out at the world is not necessarily objectively real at all. It is a perspective on reality that is constructed through a lens of ideas and attitudes that have been personally developed and culturally inherited. The assumptions beneath our thinking run so deep that we are largely not even aware of them. One trend in philosophy known as deconstructionism can be understood as the attempt to uncover the "real" truth by stripping all of our assumptions away and seeing what is left. Whatever is left is really real.

This seems unsatisfying to me because it implies that in order to find reality, we have to strip ourselves out of the picture. And that makes us, in some fundamental way, the unreal part of the universe.

There might be a better way to look at it. What would happen if we didn't define reality as what exists when we are not there, but instead assert that reality includes whatever was there before us as well as our perception of it and what we are adding?

This would mean that reality is not something separate from us that we perceive. It is a co-creative process of growth that includes the growth of our perception of it. Our perception of reality does not exist separate from reality; it is part of reality. Reality is not a static thing out there that is passively observed—it is a developing process that evolves as we do.

This evolutionary view of reality as a holistic process of growth that includes us, is central to the American philosophy called pragmatism, and I will explore some of the different aspects of that philosophy in the remaining essays of this book.

Supports my feeling that we are continuously growing and learning...

There is no end state! for Growth and learning. No end state.

Would our current journey be ruined if we remember our past journies?

" The world
doesn't just exist;
it appears to us
– and the way
it appears is not
necessarily the
way it is.

CHAPTER TWO

The Creation of Reality

As I mentioned briefly at the close of the last essay, the American philosophy of pragmatism is of particular interest to me. Pragmatism is the most significant genuinely American contribution to world philosophy. Charles Sanders Peirce and William James are generally considered to be the original founders of pragmatism, with John Dewey joining them early on and becoming the leading proponent of this way of thinking until the middle of the twentieth century.

To place the first American pragmatists in historical context, we must recognize that they were following in the footsteps of the great German idealist Immanuel Kant. In 1781 Kant published *The Critique of Pure Reason* and forever changed the world of philosophy. What Kant articulated was that reality as we perceive it is not purely pre-existent and objective; it is also, at least partly, constructed and subjective.

It is easy to believe that reality as we see it is a reflection of reality as it actually is. In short, we assume that our minds act like a mirror of reality. We tend to assume that the function that the mind plays is passive, like a mirror that doesn't alter the image of reality that it reflects. But this view of reality also leaves us disconnected from the world.

When we talk about objective reality, what we commonly mean is that which is real even if we are not around. Objective reality—the real world—is independent of us. If something is objectively real, I will see it the same way that everyone else does. If two or more people see things differently, they can't all be seeing what is objectively real. To get to what is true we would have to strip away any errors in perception or biases that any one of us might be holding. If everyone could clear their minds of biases, filters, and errors, we would all see the same truth.

That is the way we tend to think about reality. Reality, we imagine, is what is left when we are not adding anything to the picture. It already exists, and we just need to see it clearly. To get from our interpreted picture of reality to an accurate picture of reality all we need to do is strip away all of the interpretation, and then we move closer and closer to the real world. In a sense we are stripping ourselves out of the picture to find reality. But that means we exist outside of reality. Are we really outside of reality looking back at it? If we are, where are we. How can we exist outside of reality and still be real ourselves?

Kant came to the conclusion that the universe is not a static thing that sits there waiting to be discovered. It is an organic, growing thing that is created in part by us. Our perception may originate with sensations, but those sensations are ordered, organized, categorized, and ultimately shaped into reality as we perceive it. Kant was articulating a possibility for how we might have an active and creative role in the unfolding of reality.

According to Kant, there is a part of reality—the noumenon— that we can't know directly, and another part of reality—the phenomenon—that we perceive. Reality includes both. The noumenon on its own is not yet real, and perception with nothing at all behind it is not real either. Reality must include both.

Out of a myriad of physical, emotional, and conceptual sensations that enter into our awareness, we are only aware of a small part, and those are compiled into reality as we see it. The phenomenal world that we see is reality.

One of Kant's profound insights is that the picture of reality that we construct has to remain consistent through time with our previous conceptions of reality. All of the new incoming information that we receive has to be arranged in such a way that it creates a picture that does not conflict with the past. This is how we avoid ontological disorder and create a sense of unity between the present moment and all past moments. If we did not do this our experience of reality would break apart into an unintelligible chaos of random occurrences.

Kant understood human reason to be a constantly integrative process. We are bombarded with varied and largely incoherent sensations. These sensations are then filtered, ordered, and congealed into a coherent picture of reality. This consistent picture of reality Kant referred to as a "necessary transcendental unity," and he saw it as the contextual background of all of our experience. The demand that this contextual background remain coherent from moment to moment places a constant demand on the way we order our perceptions.

Kant placed human beings squarely inside of the creative process of reality. This profound connection between human perception and the creation of reality set the stage for all of Western philosophy to follow. And the American pragmatists were building on Kant's insight with the added twist that they connected reality not only to human perception, but to human activity as well. In their view, reality is in a significant way ultimately created by our actions. According to pragmatism—at least in the William James version—ideas are not true in themselves; they become true when acted upon and proven valid. Reality is created as we live it.

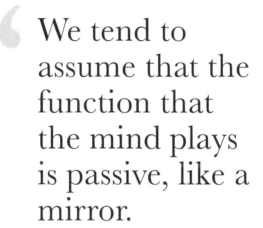

We tend to assume that the function that the mind plays is passive, like a mirror.

CHAPTER THREE

Radical Inquiry

OF ALL THE AMERICAN pragmatists Charles Sanders Peirce was following most directly along the lines of thought that had been explored by Kant. Kant, in his attempt to save the world from skepticism, insisted that there did have to be some givens—some things that we could count on—and he imagined twelve categories of such a priori or "before everything else" truths, including the laws of time, space, and causality. Peirce, like Kant, also believed that the universe had to have started with something, and one of his early attempts to identify what that something was can be found in a short paper he wrote called "Design and Chance." He read his paper on January 17, 1884, to the members of the Metaphysical Club, which he founded at Johns Hopkins University. In his paper Peirce asked fundamental philosophical questions such as, Do real things exist? and Does causality have a cause? with a wild openness that appears to be dramatically free of predispositions and preferred outcomes. His unbridled willingness to follow logic down whatever path it led, was surely the source of his creative genius.

One of the speculations Peirce offered was his certainty that someday the measurement of the angles of a triangle formed between the Earth and two distant stars would prove to us that space was, in fact, curved. Peirce insisted that the only reason we had not yet been able to confirm the curvature of space by measuring the angles of triangles was simply because we had not yet managed to measure a triangle big enough.

Peirce goes on in the paper to question the fundamental categories of reality and in particular some of those imagined by Immanuel Kant. And he did so in light of the new understanding of evolution that Darwin's recent publication of On the Origin of Species had brought to the world. The Kantian categories included space, time, and causality, and together, Kant proposed, they create a framework for what we experience as reality. Most of us assume that the universe evolved within a container of time, space, and causality, much like a calf grows to be a cow within the container of a farm. Peirce took exception to this notion. If time, space, and causality are part of an evolving universe, they must also have evolved. This deceptively simple notion may seem obvious at first glance, but its implications are enormous.

Why are moments in time ordered sequentially? Maybe the first moments appeared in random order—one now in the year 2012; the next ten days in the past; then one four months in the future; then one a thousand years in the past; and on and on. Perhaps those moments that happened by chance to appear in sequential order had a "survival advantage," and soon all of the non-sequential moments died out of existence. Maybe that is why we only find sequential moments in the universe today. And finding the universe as it is we imagine that that is how it must always have been. The same may be true with space; perhaps adjacent spots in space were not always adjacent. And again with causality, maybe things happened randomly initially, and causality only gradually developed. Peirce's radical inquiry gives us a glimpse of how much we take for granted as "real" that, when considered more deeply, turn out to be unquestioned and unproven assumptions.

What we are confronted with in Peirce's thinking could be thought of as evolutionary skepticism. Because he recognized how miniscule we are in the infinite expanse of cosmic evolution, Peirce assumed that everything we thought to be true was only relatively true—in the sense that it is true for entities of about our size, with physiological and psychological characteristics like ours, living on a planet similar to our Earth, at about this time in its history within the context of the much larger history of the universe of which it is such a tiny part.

Peirce was driven to determine what the essential characteristics of our evolving universe were. What features must have existed at the birth of the universe in order for evolution to be possible? In his inquiry Peirce identifies two absolutely necessary characteristics.

The first of these characteristics is the ability for spontaneous creation—happenings that occur by pure chance. In order for evolution to occur, Peirce realized, there must be at a bare minimum the possibility for something new to appear from nowhere and out of nothing. If this were not the case, nothing could possibly have ever arisen that could ultimately have led to the universe. But the possibility of novelty alone is not enough because any universe that contained only the ability for novelty would be doomed to total chaos. New and unrelated events would continually explode into existence in a never ending cascade of confusion. So Peirce claimed that evolution requires a second characteristic—the ability to form habits. This is the tendency for something that has already happened once to be more likely to happen again. This ten- dency toward habit assures that some degree of order will form in our universe.

So an evolving universe only requires two elements as a starting point: the ability to change and the tendency to stick. The universe is change-that-sticks. The image of evolution that Peirce evokes is one of pure possibility out of which something—and, being spontaneous, there's no telling what—bursts into being. Once "something" bursts into being it becomes more likely to happen again. Thus the universe begins its evolutionary flow that consists of events that happen by chance and then tend to happen again and again. Slowly, from nothing but possibility, the universe grows.

Mind, matter, life, nonlife is all one flowing mass of being that, at its very bottom, has only two characteristics—spontaneous chance and the tendency to form habits. Reality is a surge of existence that pours out like liquid through time. And that liquid is not equally fluid everywhere. In some places it is thin and runs like water, passing quickly from one form to another. In other places it is viscous like oil or gelatin and oozes slowly from shape to shape, remaining fixed for a time before reforming. In still others the liquid runs like glass, flowing so slowly that its movement can only be seen across vast expanses of time.

Reality is created
as we live it.

JEFF CARREIRA

Are We Outside Of Reality Looking In?

Is our experience of reality simply a perceptual illusion?

Are we outside of reality looking in?

Or is our perception of reality also part of reality?

Is the world a collection of objects that we look at from the outside?

Or is the world a flowing river of change and habit with nothing solid to it?

PART TWO

You May Not Be Who You Think You Are

We think we are a "something"—an entity that emerged in the universe on a planet called Earth. Are we really? What is a human being? What am I? Am I my body, my brain, my thoughts? Superficially, it seems that we are simply some combination of all of these things and more. When you look deeply, the simple question, Who am I? reveals mind-boggling complexity.

The following essays outline some of the ways that the American pragmatist philosophers thought about who we are.

CHAPTER FOUR:

The Stream of Consciousness

To understand the thinking of William James I have tried to see the world as I believe he saw it—as one continuous, unfolding flow. In my own contemplation of James I have followed a line of thought that mirrors in some ways his own development from a psychologist to a philosopher. James' philosophic pet peeve was any notion of duality, which means any belief in the existence of any realm of being outside of, or separate from, the rest of reality. James believed that the universe had to be one continuous, unbroken event, and he was at war with metaphysical or transcendental dualisms that allowed for two separate parts of reality to exist simultaneously. For James, mind and body, past and future, and any form of this and that, must all ultimately be part of a continuous wholeness.

In his early psychological writing James vividly described how our experience of consciousness emerges as a continuous, single stream. His conception of "the stream of consciousness" holds tremendous implications about our experience of self-consciousness and the ultimate nature of who we are.

Our experience appears to be such that while we are aware of an object we are also aware of being aware of the object. That's what it means to have self-conscious awareness and be a self-conscious entity. The same thing happens for activity. We are acting, and we are simultaneously aware that we are acting. Most of us assume that there exists both the original awareness of the object AND at the same time a simultaneous awareness of being aware of the object or of the action. Essentially we imagine a split in our consciousness. There is a "me" that is aware of the object or activity, AND another "me" that is aware of me being aware of the object or doing the activity. So where does that second "me" exist? If you think about it, you will probably realize that you don't usually think about it. If you do think about it, you might picture the awareness of yourself being aware as somehow hovering over the self that sees in the first place. The self that sees from the level of the ground so to speak, and the self that is aware of that self from some point outside. The self that is aware of ourselves is a transcendent self that exists outside of the original seeing or the original action and watches it all happen.

Because he insisted that consciousness had to be a continuous stream and that self-awareness couldn't

be separate from that stream, James concluded that
the awareness of self was simply another experience
in the ongoing flow of consciousness. Self-awareness
in this way becomes not a separate vantage point
from which to view myself viewing the object, but
rather it is just another experience in the train of experience that is all occurring in the same stream of
consciousness. At one moment I am aware only of
the object, and then in the next moment I am aware
of myself, and then in the next moment I am aware
of myself being aware of the object, and in the next
moment I am aware of the object again, and so on,
one experience after another in a continuous flow. In
this conception there is no need to imagine a transcendent self that looks down on the one who is busy
doing everything. James was happy to declare that
there is no transcendent self; there is only an experience of being aware of a sense of self that periodically
appears in the stream of consciousness.

In James' later philosophy he took this idea one
step further and stated that the world itself is created
from successive moments of experience. Experience
is the "stuff" that reality is made of. And reality, like
consciousness, appears drop by drop in one continuous stream. He didn't see ideas as existing outside of
the world pointing back at it. The physical world of
objects and the mental world of thoughts and feelings were both made up of "pure experience." Everything is pure experience. Some of those experiences

we call matter and some we call mind, but in the end the stuff that it is all made up of is pure experience.

Our awareness
of ourselves
is just another
form of
experience that
periodically
appears in
the stream of
consciousness.

CHAPTER FIVE

Process and Freewill

WILLIAM JAMES, WHO WAS trained as a medical doctor at Harvard Medical School, is often said to be America's first great psychologist. James' first and arguably most significant written work was *The Principles of Psychology*, published in 1890. James' later philosophical work always retained a certain tendency toward the psychological, and many of his core ideas were initially expressed in his earlier masterpiece.

James is famed to have been the originator of the conception of consciousness as a stream—a continuous succession of experiences. The stream of consciousness is an unending parade of thoughts, feelings, images, ideas, sensations, conceptions, emotions, and so on. Each element of experience passes before our conscious awareness and then passes away. As we discussed earlier, this view led James to a strikingly original conception of how the sense of self is formed. This view of consciousness was not without its problems, and James' lifelong project was to create a clear and comprehensive description of the process through which reality as we ex- perience it unfolds.

One of the issues that arises from the view that consciousness appears in successive chunks is explaining how we come to experience a sense of continuity between past and present moments. James recognized that the lines between the seemingly separate objects of consciousness could not be as hard-edged as we might assume. If each of our experiences was truly separate from the one that came before, it would be like living in the first moment of your life over and over and over again. You would have no memory of what came before this moment and therefore you would live in a chaos of random experiences that appeared without any connection to each other. One solution to this problem would be the existence of a transcendent self, that second "me" that we spoke about in the last chapter, the one that hovers over us and watches everything we do. That self presumably would be the one that could keep track of past events. But James was committed to explaining our experience of reality without having to resort to imagining the existence of some transcendent entity that is the other us.

James realized that there was another way to explain how the experience of continuity could exist. It is clear that instead of chaos, our experience is of a continuous stream of consciousness in which each moment of experience is immediately recognized to be part of an ongoing stream of events. James realized that this must mean that the experience of each moment must overlap with the moments behind it. Every moment has a tail that extends behind it into the past and a "fringe" that reaches ahead of it into the future. The tail and fringe of each moment overlap and cross over into the adjacent moments. In this way, our present experience includes some trace of all of the experience of the preceding moments as they trail off into the past and an anticipatory hint of all future moments as we move into them.

James explained our experience of continuity by stating that we have some sense of all past moments and anticipations of the future, but there was a second problem with this view of time—one that was very personal to James. By describing reality as a single continuous stream of experience, James did away with the need to assume the existence of any ·observer or active agent at all. What did this mean about human freewill? As a result of his own conclusions, James was forced to admit in the last chapter of *The Principles of Psychology* that as a science, psychology must assume that human experience is deterministic. In other words, human consciousness and activity flows spontaneously without there being any entity making decisions.

James was a strong libertarian and would not personally accept the determinism that even he claimed the evidence seemed to point to. He found room to insert freewill into his ideas by attributing it to the selecting function that the mind played in the process of life. He described the mind as an "organ of selection." The role that the mind played was in choosing what experiences were allowed to enter into and be held in our conscious awareness. And it was this selecting function that gave human beings what little degree of freewill we had.

In an essay entitled "Are we Automata?" James tackled the question of freewill directly. In the essay he concludes that our freedom lies in our ability to choose what we place our attention on. We all seem to have the ability through an act of will to hold our conscious attention on some thoughts to the exclusion of others. Those thoughts held firmly in consciousness will inevitably manifest in action. In this way we perform a selecting function in the stream of experience that effectively makes us the chooser of which thoughts we put our attention on and therefore which thoughts will survive in our conscious awareness long enough to generate action. This is what James called "the will to believe," and it was this ability that allowed human beings to become self-authoring.

James considered himself a moral philosopher, and he was a libertarian because he believed that our belief in freewill was required as the basis for moral action. If the world were deterministic and all of our actions were merely the natural outcome of pre- existing circumstances, how could anyone be held responsible for what they do? In his earliest professional writing, James asserts that it is our choices that define us, and ultimately what we are most responsible for is the person that we have become, a person based on the choices that we ourselves have freely made. In his book *Psychology: The Briefer Course*, James explains the ethical context for our choices:

> *The ethical energy par excellence has to . . . choose which interest out of several, equally coercive, shall become supreme. The issue here is of the utmost pregnancy, for it decides a man's entire career. When he debates, Shall I commit this crime? choose that profession? ac- cept that office, or marry this fortune?—his choice re- ally lies between one of several equally possible future Characters . . . The problem with the man is less what act he shall now resolve to do than what being he shall now choose to become.*

What we are
most responsible
for is the person
that we have
become, a
person based
on the choices
that we ourselves
have freely
made.

CHAPTER SIX

A Habit of Identification

IN THE 1870S CHARLES Sanders Peirce and William James were both members of an informal discussion circle known as the Metaphysical Club. This small group of young Harvard graduates met periodically to discuss ideas of philosophy, religion, and science in light of Charles Darwin's groundbreaking book *On the Origin of Species*, which had been published in 1859. In those meetings the ground for what would become the philosophy of pragmatism was set. John Dewey was not a member of the Metaphysical Club. Dewey was born in 1859 in Burlington, Vermont, and received his original training in philosophy at the University of Vermont where the philosophy taught was strongly influenced by another German Idealist, Georg Wilhelm Friedrich Hegel. In addition to the influence of Hegel, Dewey was also deeply intrigued by Darwin's ideas, and later when he read James' The Principles of Psychology Dewey became a converted pragmatist and would eventually become one of America's most globally influential philosophers.

James had inspired Dewey in part with his bold assertion that there was no transcendent self that acts as the observer of objects and actions. Dewey adopted James' position and took it further by admitting that there was no separate willful entity at the source of our choices and actions in a way that James himself never accepted. According to Dewey, activity happens as a response to the changing environment, not as a consequence of decisions made by a willing agent. Dewey believed that our identification with an illusionary entity called "myself" was itself merely a habit of identification.

Dewey was perplexed with James' strong libertarian belief in freewill, especially since James himself had dealt some of the hardest knocks to the notion of "the self" with his own theory of the stream of consciousness. James didn't believe that there was any "self" that existed as the observer of our experience, and yet he had insisted on reserving space for a choosing "self" to exist within the unending stream of ex- perience.

In Dewey's conception of a stream of activity, human action is explained as the unfolding of habits. There is no doer that is guiding action; there are just habitual ways of thinking and acting that have been learned in response to circumstance. As we continually engage with the environment, that encounter stimulates the formation of habits of action, thought, and emotion. As long as there is no disharmony between the environment and our habitual ways of acting, thinking, and feeling, we remain essentially unconscious.

Have you ever gotten up out of bed in the morning, made coffee, taken a shower, dressed, and left the house without really being aware of it all happening? According to Dewey, the whole process is simply a manifestation of habit. But what happens if just before we leave the house we reach into our coat pocket and realize that we don't have our car keys? At that point we become consciously aware of ourselves and the circumstances around us. There is a disharmony between the environment and our habits that blocks the habit from functioning smoothly. Something is out of place, and conscious engagement is required in order to restore the harmonious union of habit and environment.

The awakening to consciousness that occurs in the face of disharmony, according to Dewey, is an awakening to the impulse of life itself. The impediment of habit awakens us to the urgency and immediacy of life. As Dewey describes it, this awakening is not so much an awakening of a human agent to consciousness, but rather it is an awakening of the life impulse itself through the vehicle of a human form. This life impulse is directed toward the future and compelled to restore the harmony between habit and environment. In human beings this effort to restore harmony initiates a process of conscious thought in which the outcomes of different possible responses are considered until a course of action promises the satisfactory restoration of harmony. At that point an action takes place. If harmony is restored, we return again to an unconscious relationship to activity. Once we find our keys, we walk out the door and continue on unconsciously until our next encounter with disharmony.

Freedom in human activity, according to Dewey, could be increased through the expansion of our ability to think, by which he meant expanding our options for response and our ability to evaluate the relative effectiveness of different possible responses. When confronted with disharmony, the amount of freedom we will be able to exercise in response to that disharmony depends on the depth and breadth of our thought processes because more developed thinking can imagine more possible responses.

Of the early American pragmatists Dewey was arguably the most socially oriented, and he thought about social institutions, customs, and norms as habits that develop in society over time. He realized that it is the habits of society that are the active agents, not the individuals. We are not acting according to habit; habit is acting itself out through us. As he saw it, human society is a collection of habits that are continuously

acting themselves out in human form. As society develops, it is not people that are developing; it is social habits that are developing, and these habits gain expression through the actions of individuals.

Let me illustrate what Dewey was getting at with the example of the common custom of saying hello. Many people are in the habit of saying hello when they meet someone. If you ask them why they do it, they will say that it is the polite thing to do. Essentially they are stating that they are a polite person, and so they say hello because that is what polite people do. But how does the habit of saying hello develop in young children in the first place? Probably our mother, father, or other caretaker repeated the word to us over and over again. One day we successfully imitated what we heard. At that point we had no understanding of what we were saying or even that we were saying anything. We were only imitating the act of making a particular sound. When we managed to imitate the sound clearly enough, someone probably affirmed the act with affection. Through repeated reinforcement of this type, we started to develop the habit of saying hello to everyone we saw.

It was much later, once we had some mastery of language, that we learned that saying hello is polite and that we should be polite. The ideas that there are polite people, that polite people say hello, and that we are a polite person who says hello, all developed after the habit of saying hello had already been acquired. We did not start out as a self that then learned to say hello; we started as a habit of saying hello that then learned to identify itself as a person that says hello. What we call a self is really a socially constructed habit of identification.

Dewey became best known for his work in social action and education. His interest in the evolution of culture was fueled by his realization that human society develops through the formation of new cultural habits that manifest as the actions of individuals. Learning this, allowed Dewey to see that the future evolution of humanity could be guided and controlled through the conscious formation of new cultural habits, and he dedicated his life to this evolutionary calling.

What compelled Dewey most was his recognition that humanity was beginning to uncover the mechanisms through which the entire process of evolution worked. As we began to understand how the universe evolved, we could take responsibility for the future unfolding of that process. A new moral sensibility was being born as human beings became the evolutionary custodians of the future. In an essay entitled *Evolution and Ethics* Dewey describes this new moral awakening:

> *The process and the forces bound up with the cosmic have come to consciousness in man. That which was instinct in the animal is conscious impulse in man. That which was "tendency to vary" in the animal is conscious foresight in man. That which was unconscious adapta- tion and*

survival in the animal, taking place by the "cut and try" method until it worked itself out, is with man conscious deliberation and experimentation . . . Man in his conscious struggles, in his doubts, temptations, and defeats, in his aspirations and successes, is moved on and buoyed up by the forces which have developed nature; and that in this moral struggle he acts not as a mere individual but as an organ in maintaining and car- rying forward the universal process.

"
The impediment
of habit awakens
us to the urgency
and immediacy
of life.

What If You Don't Exist The Way That You've Always Thought You Did?

What if you are not a something that thinks and acts?

What if all of life were one unfolding process that included experiences of thinking, experiences of acting, and experiences of thinking that you are something that thinks and acts?

PART THREE

We Don't Know and Yet We Have To Act As If We Do

Every step we take, every action, every choice to do anything is ultimately an act of faith. Most of the time, thankfully, we live with an ongoing sense of certainty. We imagine that the world is predictable enough to support us. Then there are those moments in which everything gets swept away. We lose a job, we crash a car, a loved one passes, and we realize that nothing was ever certain. And yet we have to act as if it is or live paralyzed by doubt.

The following essays show how the American pragmatists taught us to embrace the reality of the unknown.

CHAPTER SEVEN

Fallibilism

WHAT ARE WE ASSERTING when we claim that a statement is true? What we most commonly mean is that the words we are using or the idea that we are holding in our mind correspond to some actual event or thing in the real world. This is known as the correspondence theory of truth. Implicit in this view is that there is some objective world that exists independent of our thoughts and ideas about it. If our ideas are true, then they are accurate representations of the real world. If they are false, then they are misrepresentations of the real world. The mind is seen as playing the part of a mirror that inertly reflects reality. But if this were true, how do we account for errors in thinking and judgment? A mirror never makes a mistake. If you hold a sunflower in front of a mirror, you will see a sunflower reflected in the mirror; you will never see a frog. The reflection in the mirror is always a perfect representation of what is in front of the mirror. If the mind were a simple representation-creating device, this should also be true. How do we account for the fact that we make mistakes?

One way to think about how errors occur is to realize that what we see in our minds is not just a mechanical reflection of what exists outside of our minds. It is an interpretation of what is outside of our minds. Let's throw out the metaphor of a mirror and use the metaphor of a painting. A painter can look at a landscape and recreate it on a canvas using paint. The painting will not be a perfect reflection of the scene. The quality and diversity of paint colors available and the skill of the painter are just a few of the many factors that will influence the final character of the painting and create differences between it and the landscape as viewed by the naked eye.

And so it is with the images we hold in our minds. They are not perfect reflections of the world; they are interpretations of the world. Our perceptions of the world are more like paintings that we create than reflections in a mirror. We are not passive in relationship to our perception of reality; we are partially responsible for creating it.

Central to the thinking of Charles Sanders Peirce was the belief that we could never assume that any of our perceptions or ideas were completely free of false assumptions. Our reality is built from layers of interpretation, and any errors of interpretation that exist in one layer will be transferred to the next.

Let's go back to our metaphor of a painter. Imagine that a painter paints a landscape. The landscape on the page may be beautiful, but it will not be a perfect reflection of the landscape in front of her. Now let us imagine that this painting is given to another painter who tries to paint the landscape based on what she sees in the first painting. Then that second painting is given to another painter who uses it as a model for a third painting, and so on. If we could take the one thousandth painting that was painted and bring that one back to the original landscape, I wonder how different it would be.

Peirce saw our own thoughts build in a similar way to these paintings that become models for other paintings. We see something and develop a thought about it. That thought becomes the object of another thought and that thought the object of another. This happens over and over and over again. Any preconceptions or errors in judgment get passed into future thoughts and on to other people when we communicate our ideas and perceptions to them. According to Peirce, we can never assume that what we think is an accurate reflection of reality, because no matter how hard we try to be objective we always have some errors—and probably a great deal of them—built into your thinking. Our current understanding of truth sits on a mountain of ideas and assumptions that inevitably contain innumerable inconsistencies, errors, and fallacies. No idea can ever be assumed to be true in any final sense. Peirce spoke of this principle as *fallibilism.*

Most of us feel paralyzed at the thought of being faced with this degree of uncertainty; Peirce felt the opposite. To Peirce this degree of uncertainty was the safest assumption to make. He points out that all of our knowledge is derived through the practice of generalization. In an essay called "Fallibilism, Continuity, and Evolution" he explains that all human reasoning comes through a process of "judging the proportion of something in a whole collection by the proportion found in a sample." We observe a tiny amount of the universe, and from that sample we create general ideas about what is true everywhere else. The law of gravity, as an example, was generated from watching objects fall to the earth, and it was initially assumed to be a universal law. Only later did we realize that we had made a mistake by assuming that the behavior of objects on one planet in this vast universe was typical throughout the rest of the universe. From Peirce's point of view we are one species on one planet, and that means the knowledge we have about the universe is severely limited.

Peirce was a bold and fearless inquirer partly because he had come to peace with what he saw as the extreme limitation of human understanding. We can never be absolutely certain of anything because we are always making judgments based on what we can observe, and we can never observe every possible occurrence of any phenomenon.

We experience the universe from the surface of one planet out of trillions upon trillions. We are aware of only a few thousand years of recorded history on a planet nearly five billion years old. And the tiny slice of the universe that we are aware of is seen through the very limited filter of the perceptual and intellectual apparatus of the human form.

Our attempts to understand the universe are akin to standing on a beach for a few hours peering through a drinking straw and then drawing conclusions about the nature and history of life on Earth. The sample of reality that we are able to investigate in comparison to the totality of the universe is minuscule, and so Peirce didn't presume to offer final solutions to the mysteries of existence; he only wanted to find the next best step forward for humanity to follow.

No truth should be assumed to be finally true. Truth is always in the process of building toward some final truth that we all create together. The truth as Peirce imagined it is what we are all coming to in the end. It is what will be agreed upon when every perspective and all points of view have been taken into consideration. In his review of a book called *The Works of George Berkeley*, Peirce writes:

> *There is, then, to every question a true answer, a final conclusion, to which the opinion of every man is con- stantly gravitating. He may for a time recede from it, but give him more experience*

*for consideration, and he will finally
it. The individual may not live to
truth; there is a residuum of error in
every individual's opinions. No matter; it remains that there is a definite opinion to which
the mind of man is, on the whole and in the long
run, tending.*

"We are not
passive in
relationship to
our perception
of reality; we
are partially
responsible for
creating it.

CHAPTER EIGHT

The Reality of the Unknown

IN AN ONLINE *NEW York Times* piece, the colum-
nist Errol Morris explains that there are things that
we know; there are things that we know that we don't
know; and there are things that we don't know that
we don't know. This latter group is composed of "unknown unknowns."

James, like Peirce, was very concerned with the
unknown. And like his friend he realized that humanity was adrift in a sea of unknown unknowns.
In a lecture called "Pragmatism and Religion," James
offered a metaphor to portray our true relation to the
universe:

> *I believe that we stand in much the same relation*
> *to the whole of the universe as our canine and*
> *feline pets do to the whole of human life. They*
> *inhabit our drawing rooms and libraries. They*
> *take part in scenes of whose significance they have*
> *no inkling. They are merely tangent to curves of*
> *history, the beginnings and ends and forms of*

*which pass wholly beyond their ken. So we are
tangents to the wider life of things.*

James realized that those things that "we know
that we don't know" are the limit of our imagination.
I can imagine what I don't know. I don't know many
scientific and cultural facts, the distance to the near-
est star, the president of Montenegro, and so on. But
I know there are such facts, and I readily admit to my
ignorance of them.

The unknown unknowns, on the other hand, lie
outside of my existing reference points. They are too
far out of my box to hold in mind. Take a moment to
think about it. Make a mental list of some things that
you know that you don't know. Now make a mental
list of some things that you don't know that you don't
know. It is impossible to even start that list.

The early pragmatists were very respectful of
the existence of truth beyond our current ability to
imagine. James and Peirce both assumed that what
we know about reality (and even what we can imagine about reality) is only a tiny part of the totality of
what is real. In response they created a form of inquiry and a philosophical attitude that was dramatically open-ended. "Never block the road to inquiry"
was Peirce's motto, and what he meant was that your
efforts to inquire should never lead to a point where
no further inquiry is possible. The goal of inquiry is
not to come to the end of inquiry, but to continually

open up new avenues for further investigation, because no matter what answers we find we can never
assume that they are the final truth.

James used this philosophy as the basis for out-
lining a way of life that allowed us to effectively live
in the unknown. To function in a universe so radi-
cally full of uncertainty, the first thing that we must
do is liberate our thinking, and one of the ways that
our thinking gets stuck is through a process James
called "vicious intellectualism." Using this term
James described how our concepts about reality can
hinder the process of inquiry if we believe that they
represent actual reality. Human beings create concepts. When we recognize something to be real or
true, we label it with a word or an idea. We concep-
tualize. Once a concept is created we tend to believe
in the truth of that concept and simultaneously assume that anything that contradicts it must be false.
If I see something and believe that it is a cat, I always
believe at the same time that it is not a dog, a mouse,
or a fire truck. In my mind the positive assertion of
something being a cat includes the negative assertion
of it not being a dog, a mouse, a fire truck, or anything else. What if we are talking about the concept
of God? If we hold one conception of "God" to be
true, then we will simultaneously assume that every
other definition of God is false. James realized that
when talking about more subtle and significant concepts this habit of vicious intellectualism causes big

trouble—as in, "My definition of God is true, and therefore yours must be false."

James' notion of vicious intellectualism can be understood as the assumption that the way we see things, is the way they actually are. What James meant by vicious intellectualism is similar to what Wilfrid Sellars meant by the myth of the given. The reason he was so concerned about it was because he saw how our ability to inquire is profoundly impaired by the negating assumptions that get smuggled into our thinking.

We never think to question these unconscious negations because they are hidden from view deep inside our positive assertions. And if we fail to question our concepts we tend to follow paths of inquiry that can only proceed by expanding on what is already known. In James' opinion we hold so tightly to whatever truth we believe we have already come to, that we are only willing to inquire at the borders of what we already know. This is how we avoid having to face the vast ocean of unknown unknown that always surrounds our tiny island of knowledge.

The philosophy of pragmatism was meant to offer a different approach to inquiry. In pragmatic inquiry, truth is not seen as a collection of knowable facts, but rather as an ongoing process of investigation. No truth should be considered final; all truth is the jumping off point to further investigation because whatever we think is true today will inevitably yield to a bigger and more encompassing conception of truth tomorrow. For James that meant developing the willingness to inquire directly into what we don't already know by focusing on the anomalies and the oddities that we can't comprehend because they don't fit into our current understanding of reality.

James wanted to focus more attention on the vast outer reaches thet always exist far from what we know. The next big idea doesn't come from the center of what we already know—it comes from the dim outer edge, where the light of what we know fades into the blackness of the unknown unknowns beyond. James risked his career and his reputation as an academic and a scientist to study things that others thought were absurdities. As president of the Society for Psychical Research, he studied spirits, mediums, and life after death. Most scientists felt that studying these strange, unexplainable phenomena was a waste of time because they took us too far from what we already knew to be true and left us with know reasonable means of validation. James, on the other hand, felt that they were the first place we should look because they already proved that whatever we know isn't enough.

"The goal of inquiry is not to come to the end of inquiry, but to continually open up new avenues for further investigation ...

CHAPTER NINE

Evolutionary Existentialism

Peirce and James were lifelong friends and colleagues who were busy with two complimentary, but distinctly different philosophical agendas. Peirce's philosophical aspiration was to lay down the foundation for a philosophical system that could explain the existence and evolution of everything. He complained later in his life that James had taken the philosophy of pragmatism and anchored it too narrowly to merely human concerns. James was concerned with explaining our human experience of life and developing a philosophy that would allow us to act with confidence in spite of the unavoidable insecurities we faced.

To understand James it is important to recognize that his concerns were existential. The characteristic that most unifies existentialists is their belief that human beings must look squarely into the ultimate mysterious emptiness that lies at the core of reality. In the face of this overwhelming uncertainty we must not cower or turn our heads toward the past. Truth is not something you search for. It is not a hidden treasure to find. Truth to an existentialist is something you stand for—a stake that each of us must plant firmly for ourselves in the face of doubt. The future is not waiting to be discovered; it is what we will build together through the individual stands that we take.

In his book *Irrational Man,* William Barrett comments that "of all non-European philosophers William James probably best deserves to be labeled an Existentialist." Barrett goes on to assert that it would be more accurate to call James an existentialist than a pragmatist. Indeed, many of the themes and concerns that occupy James' philosophy are those that also occupied the European existentialists, not the least of which was his defense of faith. James took on a powerful scientific world and risked his own reputation by defending the right to believe even without direct evidence. James' essay "The Will to Believe" was his manifesto on the necessity of faith.

In his defense of faith James was challenging a philosophical position known as *logical positivism.* You and I and almost anyone likely to read this book is probably at heart a logical positivist without even knowing it. In fact, for most of us anything else is hard to relate to. Logical positivism dictates that something is only true if there is conclusive evidence that demonstrates it to be true. In other words, truth has to be proven before it is accepted. Nothing should be accepted on faith.

James questioned this view. Is it possible to wait for conclusive evidence before we believe in something? Why do we think that conclusive evidence is the best way to know what is true? James believed that ultimately truth had to be a matter of faith. Even the position of logical positivism was a matter of faith in the end, because the idea that waiting for conclusive evidence is the best way to validate truth is itself taken on faith.

There is so much that we see as reality that is actually nothing more than unquestioned beliefs that we have unconsciously accepted on faith. James realized that these deep beliefs often don't result from evidence. Consciously or unconsciously we are choosing to believe in these ideas and then acting as if they were true. We are, in effect, staking our lives on them. These assumptions might have been handed to us by our culture; they might have been dictated by religion; or they might have come from experiences in our own life—most likely a combination of all three. Rest assured, however, somewhere underneath everything there are many presumptions about reality that you accept as true without conclusive evidence and perhaps without even realizing it. We are very often acting on faith.

As James saw it, whatever we choose to believe in, or choose not to believe in, will affect the way we act and live, so how we exercise our "will to believe" is of the utmost importance. We stand on our beliefs, and from there we push off into an uncertain future where the results of our actions will either strengthen our confidence in our beliefs or force us to reconsider them. Rather than holding back and waiting for proof, James prefers to lean forward into life, accepting the reality that many of our decisions must be made on faith, doing our best to consciously choose what to believe, and then acting wholeheartedly as if the truth of those beliefs were assured. The process of human life is then a relentless affair of jumping consciously yet somewhat blindly into the future and then continually adjusting and readjusting our beliefs based on the results.

In his essay "Great Men and Their Environment," James directly examines the evolutionary significance of our choices. As he sees it, the people we become through our conscious choices can act as guideposts that lead the evolution of our culture forward. He opens the essay with the question, "What are the causes that make communities change from generation to generation?" And he concludes that, "The difference is due to the accumulated influences of individuals, of their examples, their initiatives, and their decisions." James' brand of evolutionary existentialism rests on the conscious exercise of our will to believe. By choosing which ideas to believe in and then acting on them, we can embody new possibilities for human existence. Once embodied these possibilities either compel others to adopt them or are rejected and disappear. The evolution of society occurs as embodied ideas enter into a natural process of cultural selection. Great individuals embody or, as Emerson would have said, "represent," possibilities that the rest of humanity follow until they become cultural norms. We can take an increasingly active part in this process by becoming more consciously aware of the beliefs that we are choosing to believe in and embody.

JEFF CARREIRA

"The idea that waiting for conclusive evidence is the best way to validate truth is itself taken on faith.

Human life is a risk

To believe in anything is a risk.

To not believe is also a risk.

Anything we do is a risk.

Not doing anything is also a risk.

We might decide to avoid all risk by believing nothing and doing nothing.

That is very risky.

Better to believe and act wholeheartedly, always ready to think again and change our minds.

JEFF CARREIRA

PART FOUR

The Circumstances Around Us Are Changing Faster Than We Can

The world and everything in it is changing all the time, and our beliefs about it all must change at least as quickly. Often they don't.

We often find ourselves stuck in beliefs whose time has passed, not knowing which questions to ask or what direction to take forward.

These concluding essays outline the evolutionary challenge of our time and the role that philosophical inquiry can play in meeting that challenge.

JEFF CARREIRA

CHAPTER TEN

Our Evolutionary Crisis

What is a crisis? I would propose that a crisis occurs when the circumstances around us are changing more rapidly than we can change in response. When we find ourselves in crisis, we are overwhelmed by circumstances that are changing faster than we can, and we are called upon to find an extraordinary means of response.

The awareness of a crisis tends to bring with it a sense of panic and an associated desperation for immediate action. Under such circumstances we are tempted to disregard philosophical considerations even though they are often at the heart of the original reasons for the crisis. The twentieth-century anthropologist and philosopher Gregory Bateson has provocatively stated that:

> *The major problems in the world are the result of the difference between the way nature works and the way man thinks.*

We base our actions on our understanding of the nature of reality and the way the world works. That understanding is partly made up of our consciously held beliefs about what is true, but much more so by unconsciously held convictions that we are not even aware we have. To the extent that our convictions about what is true are inaccurate we will find ourselves unable to respond appropriately to our challenges and problems. And it is the work of philosophical introspection that allows us to bring awareness to our unconscious assumptions so that they may be examined, altered, or discarded completely.

Many of our world's greatest challenges are symptoms of an overarching evolutionary crisis. This overarching crisis is caused by the fact that the circumstances of our world are changing at a faster and faster pace, and human beings are not able to keep up. Our problems seem to be compounding because we are not able to respond adequately to one crisis before the next one arises, and then there is another and another. We sometimes feel like we are being buried under a pile of insurmountable problems.

No one solution to any given problem is going to remedy this situation. What needs to change is our ability to respond—our response-ability. Human beings need to learn how to respond faster. We have to learn to uncover unconscious assumptions, examine them, and then change the way we act with greater and greater speed and efficiency. We must all become high-speed, super-efficient philosophers and accelerating change agents. In times of crisis, especially evolutionary crisis, philosophy is far from a luxury.

To increase the rate at which we change, we need to examine our relationship to the feeling of change. Isn't it true that we have all been conditioned to experience trepidation—ranging from anxiety to terror—whenever we encounter a new situation or circumstance? We have been conditioned to be cautious of anything new, which leads us to avoid change. In order for us to be able to keep up with our world's accelerating rate of change, one of the first things that we need to change is the way we feel about change.

For thousands of years human beings believed that the universe was fundamentally unchanging. It was a static stage upon which the drama of life played out. In such a universe "change" feels "bad." If things are supposed to remain fixed, then any time we feel things changing we instinctively feel fear and insecurity—something is wrong. Isn't that what happens? When things start to change, don't you get uneasy, don't your alarm bells start to ring? We are conditioned to fear change.

Now that we realize we live in an evolutionary universe and that we as a human family need to evolve, we must learn to feel uneasy when things don't change. Imagine traveling in a train. If it comes to a halt in the middle of the tracks, you get uneasy and imagine that something is wrong because the train is supposed to move. An evolutionary universe is also supposed to move. We need to develop a more positive sensibility toward experiences of change so that we won't automatically recoil from change and miss important opportunities for growth as a result.

What needs
to change is
our ability to
respond – our
response—ability.

JEFF CARREIRA

CHAPTER ELEVEN

Philosophy Is Not a Luxury

THE PREMISE OF THIS book is that philosophy is not a luxury item that we can afford to do away with. It is a necessity for a well-lived human life—especially when we are challenged, or worse, when we find ourselves in times of crisis.

When we face mounting challenges and overwhelming crises, we are tempted to see philosophy as a luxury item that we can no longer afford. It's not! In fact, in the face of overwhelming difficulties, philosophy, which is the pursuit of truth, becomes more important, not less.

Why? Because what we believe is true dictates how we act, and how we act creates the world we live in.

If you recognize some part of yourself that protests against this statement, look at it. It might be insisting that, "My actions are not dictated to me. I do what I want to do. I am a free, independent person."

Most of us believe that nothing can dictate our actions to us—not even our own beliefs. What if it isn't true? What if you were to discover that you could only ever act in accordance with what you believed to be true—that you were a prisoner of your own beliefs and always would be? How would you relate to philosophy and to your quest to examine what is true then?

I'm not ready to go so far as to say that there is no freewill, but I do appreciate James' insight that our freedom is not found in our ability to choose our actions, but in our ability to choose what we believe. James, like Dewey, also recognized that the world we create as a society depends on the truths we share in society. These words from James' essay *The Will to Believe* still have something powerful to say to us today:

> *A social organism of any sort whatever, large or small, is what it is because each member proceeds to his own duty with a trust that the other members will simultaneously do theirs. Wherever a desired result is achieved by the cooperation of many independent persons, its existence as a fact is a pure consequence of the precursive faith in one another of those immediately concerned. A government, an army, a commercial system, a ship, a college, an athletic team, all exist on this condition, without which not only is nothing achieved, but nothing is even attempted.*

If we agree that the world is created by the results of our individual and collective actions, and we know that the world needs to change, then we have to discover a new truth together. Philosophy, as the pursuit of truth, is critical and must become a collective endeavor so that we can change the world by changing the way we think about the world.

Times of crisis are times when we need to focus our attention and our energy. Some things that were important to us before become luxuries that we can no longer afford. Philosophy is not one of these. In times of crisis more than ever, we must examine what we believe to be true and why we believe it, so we can discover higher, deeper, and more encompassing truths that will lead to actions that will change the world for the better.

"We can change the world by changing the way we think about the world.

What Beliefs Are You Holding On To Right Now?

What beliefs are you holding onto right now?

How are you evaluating the validity of those beliefs?

Are you ready to let them go when it's time to change?

About the Author

JEFF CARREIRA IS A meditation teacher, mystical philosopher and author who teaches to a growing number of people throughout the world. As a teacher, Jeff offers retreats and courses guiding individuals in a form of meditation he refers to as The Art of Conscious Contentment. Through this simple and effective meditation technique, Jeff has led thousands of people in the journey beyond the confines of fear and self-concern into the expansive liberated awareness that is our true home.

Ultimately, Jeff is interested in defining a new way of being in the world that will move us from our current paradigm of separation and isolation into an emerging paradigm of unity and wholeness. He is exploring some of the most revolutionary ideas and systems of thought in the domains of spirituality, consciousness, and human development. He teaches people how to question their own experience so deeply that previously held assumptions about the nature of reality fall away to create space for dramatic shifts in understanding.

Jeff is passionate about philosophy because he is passionate about the power of ideas to shape how we perceive reality and how we live together. His enthusiasm for learning is infectious, and he enjoys addressing student groups and inspiring them to develop their own powers of inquiry. He has taught

JEFF CARREIRA

students at colleges and universities throughout the world.

Jeff is the author of numerous books including: *The Art of Conscious Contentment, No Place But Home, The Miracle of Meditation, The Practice of No Problem, Embrace All That You Are, Philosophy Is Not a Luxury, Radical Inclusivity, The Soul of a New Self,* and *Paradigm Shifting.*

For more about Jeff or to book him for a speaking engagement, visit: jeffcarreira.com

Made in United States
Orlando, FL
28 May 2022

18285529R00085